Other Books by Elaine Reeder

You Mean The World To Me
From Our Home To Yours
The Boss's Right Arm
Side By Side in the South Pacific
Side By Side in SE Asia & Australia
Side By Side in Scotland
Side By Side in the Caribbean

Our Guiding Light

Spiritual Poems in Times of Need

Elaine Reeder

Special Edition Publishing
Edmonton, Alberta, Canada

Copyright © Elaine Reeder 2004, 2007

Printed by ScanCopy Print Inc
Edmonton, Alberta,Canada

Illustrations & Cover by Jan Vandenberg

Library and Archives Canada Cataloguing in Publication

Reeder, Elaine, 1950-
  Our guiding light: spiritual poems in times of need/ Elaine Reeder.

ISBN 0-9687648-5-1

1.Christian poetry, Canadian (English) 2. Bereavement—Poetry. I. Title.

PS8585.E38097 2004   C811'.54   C2004-903359-X

Special Edition Publishing
3260 – 38 Ave, Edmonton, Alberta, Canada
780-440-0632

In memory of our loved ones
living eternally with our
Heavenly Father

Table of Contents

God's Love In Humanity

But Are We So Different?

There are so many differences
In the world today
Many find it tough
To go the right way.

Our clothing is different
We don't speak the same
Some make it to the top
Through fortune and fame.

Our lifestyles are different
We don't see eye to eye
No common courtesy
We don't even try.

Our education is different
From place to place
Our standards are different
From race to race.

Our ethnic bodies
Stand proud and tall
Announcing to the world
We're the best of all.

Our neighborhoods are different
We don't have the same taste
In communities of aplenty
So much goes to waste.

Our expectations are different
In parts that are global
We all want to feel
Others will be noble.

And when it comes down to
The color of ones skin
That's where we should start
Where we should begin.

For it matters not if we're
Yellow, black or white
Who's to say our way
Is wrong or right.

Although our beliefs may be different
We have one common bond
Our creator of this world
Of Him we are so fond.

Creatures Of Habit

We're creatures of habit
We don't like to change
We like things the same
Not be rearranged.

When progress steps in
We say oh no or nay
We'll just keep doing it
The same old way.

We like the feeling of comfort
Of things staying the same
Not having to think
Or no one to blame.

But when health declines
We just can't believe
Additives put in food
Were in to deceive.

And when a crisis occurs
A loved one taken
The pattern's been broken
We feel forsaken.

Change is not easy
To leave behind the past
But new habits can form
And they too shall last.

Change can compare
Like day into night
Like Summer into Fall
Like darkness into light.

Change can be good
Like colored leaves in Fall
Or new buds in Spring
With a purposeful call.

Or like the caterpillar
Taking on a new form
Becoming something special
Different from the norm.

But we too can change
If we so desire
Get rid of bad habits
Before we retire.

Take a good look
At what you can improve
Areas of your life
Stuck in the old groove.

Take decisive action
On what you can change
Pull out all the stops
On the barrier range.

If forgiveness is needed
Try letting it go
If restraint in spending
To credit say no.

A healthier diet
And exercise too
May be 'round the corner
Just waiting for you.

No, change isn't easy
It's effort and work
But the feeling inside
Is the greatest perk.

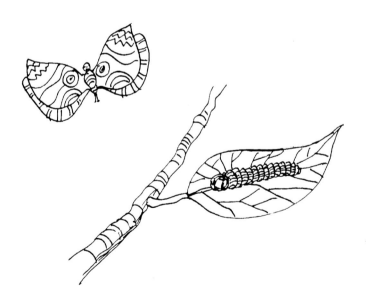

Stepping Into Another's Shoes

Before we complain, criticize or defile
We must walk in another's shoes for awhile
To get a real feel for someone's life
We must pick up his staff and work his strife.

We must reach deep inside to feel his pain
Then there'll be no reason for scorn or disdain
For out of our hearts will pour compassion
In a gentle flow but stately fashion.

For God steps in when we are caring
Extending His love through us by sharing
He softens our hearts with one swift motion
Replacing hardheartedness or any cruel notion.

By giving to us, we can give to others
By loving our neighbors just like our brothers
No need for jealousy, envy or resentment
For where love is, there's only contentment.

Stepping into another's shoes, even for a minute
Can release boundaries surpassing the limit
It's God's everlasting love giving us strength
To reach eternal life by going the extra length.

The Path Less Traveled

Most people travel
The path of least resistance
They go the easy way
At everyone's insistence.

They bet on the sure thing
Never taking a risk
Or if they do
Others shake their heads tsk tsk.

Some people don't want you
To get ahead or succeed
They're only too happy
When you fail or recede.

Jealousy is a disease
Harbored to no end
Our dreams and goals
Shouldn't have to bend.

For what is truly
In our hearts and minds
Can be achieved
With faith which binds.

The path less traveled
Has greater rewards, by far
Have strong convictions
When others hinder or mar.

They're setting up roadblocks
To test your faith and strength
To see if you can go
The distance and the length.

You cannot be swayed
If your belief is strong
In your heart you know
It can't be wrong.

Don't be afraid
To take the path less traveled
Prayers will be answered
And questions unraveled.

Our Lord will be watching
As you go on your way
He's always there for you
At the end of the day.

Who Are The Most Afflicted?

Who are the most afflicted
In this world of today?
Is it the ones with labels
Or those going the wrong way?

Is it the darkness of the blind
Those that cannot see
Or the gifted sight-full
Not being all they could be?

Is it the silence of the deaf
Those that cannot hear
Or the alert intellect
Stunted by his own fear?

Is it the quietness of the mute
Those that cannot speak
Or the talkative braggart
Who within himself is weak?

Is it the immobility of the crippled
Those that cannot walk
Or the shifting transients
At positive thoughts balk?

What good are two eyes
If you're looking the wrong way?
What good are two ears
If you're scared every day?

What good are two lips
If you're lacking self-esteem?
What good are two legs
If you're lacking a dream?

Are you the unlabeled afflicted
In this world of today
Make your choices wisely
And go the right way.

What Is Success?

Success doesn't come in a bottle
With a special formula inside
Nor with fancy packaging
Or instructions as a guide.

Success doesn't come in a jar
Or taste as sweet as honey
It isn't about expensive cars
Or having lots of money.

Success can't be bought
Or even given away
It seems to be out there
If we're willing to pay.

But how do we get it
If it's not to be seen
How will others know
Not seeing where we've been?

Must we prove to others
We're better than the rest
Must we keep striving
To be good, better, best?

Can't we be satisfied
Without proving wealth
Focusing instead
On well-being and health.

Success is in the mind
Of every human being
It's a matter of priorities
Of what we're really seeing.

Success can be small things
Like greeting a brand new day
Putting on a smile
To help others along the way.

Success is carrying yourself
Upright and tall
It's picking yourself up
When you've taken a fall.

Success is feeling good
When others doom you wrong
Sticking to your principles
Can make you grow strong.

Success is deep inside
Belief system intact
It doesn't depend on
How others will react.

Success is using talents
Developed or God-given
Shared with those abound
Or those less driven.

Success is a warm fuzzy feeling
A glow you can't hide
Success is so much more
Than words can describe.

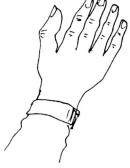

It's Never Too Late

It's never too late
To spread your wings and fly
Don't be a wingless bird
Let the wind carry you high.

Don't be afraid of new heights
Let your new self emerge
Wear a confident smile
Let your energy serge.

Walk with intention
Put a skip in your stride
Let others follow
Be their model and guide.

Chase the blues away
Whistle a happy tune
It's a brand new era
Shed that old cocoon.

Be a beautiful butterfly
On a mission of your own
Create a symphony
Set your own tone.

Choose your own palette
It's never too late
To be who you are
No need to wait.

Principles Of Success

No greater power
Hath our minds over thee
Willing our bodies forward
To be all we can be.

With definitive purpose
And goals in our heads
A positive mental attitude
Binding the threads.

A pleasing personality
And enthusiasm to the core
Gives energy to teamwork
To go one mile more.

Self-discipline, controlled attention
And learning from defeat
Can add to creative vision
On what we want to beat.

It takes personal initiative
To allocate money or time
For ultimate achievements
We need to be in our prime.

With applied faith
And using the cosmic force
Whatever our minds believe
Will keep us on the course.

For there is no other
Exactly like you or me
And in all of eternity
There never will be.

Use the power of the mind
For only positive and good
And ye shall be rewarded
As rightly you should.

Born To Be Champions

No matter what obstacles
Or difficulties lie along the way
We were born to be champions
And have victory one day.

The world keeps changing
Whether or not we choose
But with definitive purpose
We cannot purposely lose.

It starts with a goal
Or a clear-cut picture
Add some positive thinking
To the formula mixture.

By visualizing the picture
The mind goes to work
Creating enthusiasm
As an additional perk.

More thinking and enthusiasm
Turn into burning desire
It could trigger an idea
To take off like wild fire.

By naming our goals
Getting on the right track
We can enjoy many advantages
There's nothing we lack.

By knowing what we want
Looking in the right section
There are more opportunities
Headed in our direction.

We were born with a mind
All the faculties we need
Everyone has talents
In order to succeed.

Inspirational Dissatisfaction

What do you do
When you make a mistake
When things go wrong
And they seem half-baked?

What do you do
When you face defeat
Everything seems black
You feel totally beat?

When it appears
There's no way to turn
An opportunity occurs –
A chance to learn.

Don't become frightened
Give up or run away
Face your adversity
Be strong-willed and stay.

For when you develop
Inspirational dissatisfaction
You also develop faith,
Clear thinking and positive action.

Inspirational dissatisfaction
Can motivate to success
In every achievement
The Lord is there to bless.

For every major difficulty
There's a silver lining inside
Waiting for you to find it
Whenever you decide.

So seize the moment
Of divine discontent
Change your circumstances
For it is Heaven sent.

It can change poverty to riches
Failure to success
Defeat to victory
Misery to happiness.

Inspirational dissatisfaction
Is positive, it's true
Making a special difference
In the world around you.

So Many Shoes

We've all heard the expression
Walk a mile in my shoes
So come with me on a journey
What have you got to lose?

Let's step into some shoes
And see how they must fit
Will we be able to walk a mile
Or maybe just a bit?

Some shoes are very big
And not easy to fill
They take responsibility
Have plenty of strong will.

Then there are small shoes
Tiny shoes taking baby steps
Wobbly, unsure at times
Yet no fear of depths.

There are wide shoes and narrow shoes
And others in-between
Pinching shoes, ill-fitting shoes
And some just peachy keen.

There are comfortable shoes
The ones we like to keep
They have durable qualities
Not tossed in a heap.

Casual shoes say I'm carefree
Dressy shoes say I'm classy
Loafers say I'm weary
Runners – I'm an active lassie.

The kind of shoe you put on
Tells the story of your roots
Doesn't matter if you don
Dancing slippers or cowboy boots.

It takes a mighty person
From the toe to the heel
To slip on another's shoes
And see how they must feel.

Not all will be the comfy ones
Some will rub the wrong way
But thank you for coming along
On this journey today.

Starving For Love

Famine isn't just about food
Some people are starving for love
They want that fuzzy feeling
Of a partner who fits like a glove.

Some people are so hungry
They look in the wrong places
They get used and abused
And fall flat on their faces.

They turn to the wrong people
To get an emotional high
Then are disappointed
And wondering why.

In today's world it's hard
To find a good match
On all types of levels
To connect – to attach.

Some people only look
For a physical attraction
A part of the equation
But only a fraction.

On a mental level
It's important to communicate
When decisions come up
You'll need to adjudicate.

Emotionally there's nothing better
Than someone who can understand
How you feel inside your heart
Whether it is grieving or grand.

But the most important of all
Is to connect on a spiritual level
For in God's eyes
This is where we truly revel.

When we can pray together
Be loving, kind and sweet
That's when our needs will be met
And our hearts really meet.

Being Different

What is so wrong
With being different from the rest?
Why do we think uniformity
Is parallel to the best?

Haven't we all experienced
Discrimination at some time
Either too young or too old
Are we ever in our prime?

Is the world for Joe Average
Not too short or too tall
Not too rich or too poor
Somewhere half way up the wall?

Can't be too masculine for a woman
Or too feminine for a male
Can't have our skin too dark
Nor bleached albino pale.

Do we all have to land
Squarely in the middle
To be accepted by the world
In this glorious riddle?

What is so wrong with
Being different from the rest
Are we so afraid to stand out
To take the challenge or the test?

Are we afraid to stand up
To be proud of who we are
Cowering in the background
Instead of reaching afar.

None of us are perfect
We all have our little quirks
But gather up your talents
And use whatever works.

To be successful at life
A genius – no need to be
For even a fool knows
His choice of actions is free.

There's really nothing wrong
With having a different form
A different color or look
Pray tell what is the norm?

For it matters little
When we come to God's door
If we are short or tall
Or rich or poor.

He'll be looking at our record
How we valued our life
Did we achieve success
In spite of our strife?

Did we use our uniqueness
To make a world of difference
Or sit back in the shadows
With our imperfect inference?

Did we let the negative
Hold us back
Or turn it around
And counter attack?

There's nothing wrong
With being different from the rest
It could be God's blessing
Working His miracle best.

God's Love In Spirituality

Our Guiding Light

I know it's not often easy
To choose the right path to go
With so many diversions out there
It's really hard to know.

We're so easily drawn into
The latest gadgets of the day
And so busy with activities
We forget to stop and pray.

We're so all consumed
With being bigger, better, best
We lose sight of the right path
And get bogged down with the rest.

It's time for us to slow down
And to pick up the Holy Book
For our guiding light is there
If we'd only stop and look.

The guiding light shines forth
For all those willing to see
It serves as a directional map
For the likes of you and me.

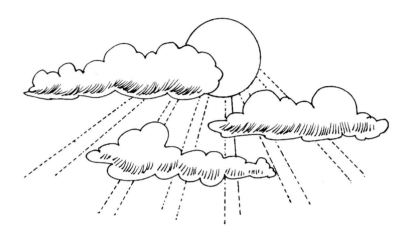

Our guiding light gives us freedom
To enjoy with peace of mind
The fruits of God's labor
And the love that we find.

If we look for the genuine
The simple, the true and pure
The right path will stand out
It will be lit; that's for sure.

Jesus, A Carpenter's Son

Jesus was a carpenter's son
His disciples, fishermen of the sea
He turned them into fishers of men
Simple people like you and me.

He preached not on a pulpit
But sometimes high upon a rock
It mattered little of place
Throngs came to hear Him talk.

He healed the crippled and blind
Cast out demons one by one
He traveled from town to town
His work was never done.

He had no belongings
Only the clothes upon His back
His followers were poor in riches
But in spirit they did not lack.

He taught in story form
Parables, they were called
It was easier to understand
As they sat quietly enthralled.

They had many lessons to be learned
In the olden days of yore
But has it changed so very much
Are we still living as before?

Has our faith in Jesus been cast aside
In favor of chance winnings
How can we be so blind
When He provides new beginnings?

Our lot is not cast by luck
Our choices have been made
Whether right or wrong
The pathway has been laid.

No turning back to undo
All the mistakes along the way
But asking for forgiveness
Can start a brand new day.

He was brought here for a reason
Just as you and I
Are we living to our potential
Or just getting by?

Our Relationship With Jesus

Our relationship with Jesus
Is as important as can be
No greater man ever lived
Nor ever will be as He.

God blessed us with life
Then gave us free will
To do so as we wished
But be accountable still.

He gave us special talents
That we could all embrace
But if we didn't use them
Could not go back and erase.

The belief in a higher power
Was taught by His only Son
A prayer to the Heavenly Father
Thy kingdom come, Thy will be done.

So in our time spent
Between birth and death
What is the real purpose
Of what He bequeath?

He wanted us to know His Son
Whether here or in Heaven
Make it known to us
He's available twenty-four seven.

Getting to know Jesus
On a personal level
Would please God
Beyond the words of revel.

He's easy to get to know
Through the Bible it is written
And once you read about Him
Will become more than smitten.

His love for all mankind
Overflowed past the brim
Everlasting love
Eternally from Him.

Who would give His life
Such an unselfish act
For the benefit of others
It is written as a fact.

He came to save our souls
To give everlasting life
To give our existence meaning
To ease the pain and strife.

He came to give us hope
Our efforts were not in vain
His words were of God
There was knowledge to gain.

Our relationship with Jesus
Is important as can be
No greater man ever lived
Nor ever will be as He.

My Love For Jesus

My love for Jesus
Is like a songbird in Spring
It's like the melodic sounds
When the church bells ring.

My love for Jesus
Is like a river flowing
Ever constant, never changing
Never ebbing, never slowing.

My love for Jesus
Is like a mountain peak
The highest of the pinnacles
Of whatever I may seek.

My love for Jesus
Is like a fragrant flower
He fills my lungs with air
And turns on spiritual power.

My love for Jesus
Is solid as a rock
The strength I draw from Him
To talk the talk and walk the walk.

I Am A Beacon Of Light

I am a beacon of light
Shining example to see
From within comes truth
No greater love has He.

I am a beacon of light
Spreading far and wide
Giving hope to others
To be by His side.

I am a beacon of light
Values held in high esteem
Not to be diminished
Brightness in every beam.

I am a beacon of light
Attracting those in need
Giving comfort and love
And planting the seed.

I am a beacon of light
Directing those home
Giving them a path
So they won't have to roam.

Jesus Is Like A Lighthouse

Jesus is like a lighthouse
Guiding the way
Showing us the path
To avoid rocks in the bay.

In the darkest hour
His beam shines strong
He shows there's hope
When everything's gone wrong.

His bright light reaches
Every corner of the earth
Casting rays continually
On each and every birth.

So pure is the radiance
None other can compare
Crucial in stormy weather
Tranquil in waters fair.

He stands tall and erect
For all to see
He wants us to know
He's there for you and me.

Be Careful What You Sow

Be careful what you sow
In getting to the top
If it's purely for adulation
You may be headed for a flop.

Not all of us will make the pinnacle
Just like when sowing some seeds
Some may fall among thorns
And be choked by the weeds.

Some may fall by the wayside
Eaten by birds the next day
Some may fall by the rocks
And just wither away.

But ones planted in good soil
Spring up double-fold
Strong in belief
With a sturdy foothold.

Don't be self-absorbed
In riches or pleasures of life
Don't have energies scattered
Compounding errors with rife.

Don't give up quickly
When things go the wrong way
Stick with it; proceed
Till the end of the day.

Every seed planted in good soil
Growing closer to your choice
Will be following the path
Of a Superior voice.

41

The Treasures In Heaven

Why are we never satisfied
With what we have, the lot
We go and buy more
Just after we've bought.

We never have enough
It's way beyond need
Over-abundance of things
Could be called greed.

What compels us to gather
And round up more stuff
When there's billions of people
Who have it more rough.

Do we think God will care
If we drive a bigger car
Have an executive office
Or become a movie star?

Will He be taking inventory
While us in our haste
Consume more products
To discard and waste?

Can't we be satisfied
With what we've got
Did we totally forget
What Jesus taught?

Those with unbridled wealth
Will despair the day
At the door of God's house
When they have to pay.

Easier for a camel
Through the eye of a needle
Than enter God's kingdom
With conniving and wheedle.

For many who are first
Will now go last
Their greed for possessions
Will haunt their past.

The treasures in Heaven
Are worth so much more
Than spending on ourselves
And neglecting the poor.

Love In Any Language

Countries have their mother tongue
But we're not really worlds apart
For love in any language
Is spoken from the heart.

Sometimes words aren't needed
To convey what's deep inside
For when love flows unconditionally
There's no need to confide.

Governments try to separate
Divide, conquer and fall
But love brings us together
And tears down the wall.

Unyielding keeps us at odds
Compromising closes the gap
But love goes above and beyond
It gives us a cosmic zap.

We have too much in common
To let differences be unresolved
We were all created equally
But somehow jealousy evolved.

We may be different colors
I know we're all unique
But love in any language
Is what the heart will speak.

An Angel Upon My Shoulder

I've got an angel upon my shoulder
Advising me what to do
I'm sure I'm not the only one
I bet you've got one too.

They can see so much further
Of what lies ahead
They can steer us in different directions
Of what we fear or dread.

They are so very pleased with us
When warnings are heeded
We appreciate their guidance
Their help is greatly needed.

And when we choose not to listen
Then stumble and fall
They still remain there for us
For our every beck and call.

So for all the angels out there
Doing good deeds today
Let's give them a round of applause
And a big hip-hip hurray!

Jesus Spoke

Jesus spoke in parables
So His followers would know
The glories of His kingdom
And how they could grow.

He touched on many subjects
Pertinent to their life
He enlightened their minds
And eased their strife.

He guided them towards
The truth of the Lord
And through it all
Much love He poured.

For His love of the people
Carried Him through
The persecution and death,
The rising anew.

The Prophesy Fulfilled

I know the prophesy
Had to be fulfilled
But oh so merciless
The way He was killed.

My heart weeps for Him
At thought of the scourging
While contempt for soldiers
Whose power was surging.

How dare they spat on
The Son of God
Then taunt Him, mock Him
And raise the rod.

I feel so ashamed
Humans would do such
To our Lord, our God
Who did so much.

He healed, He taught
He forgave their sin
He spoke of salvation
And to believe in Him.

They wanted Him crucified
The people in the crowd
"Release the murderer,"
They shouted out loud.

So they hauled Him away
And beat Him some more
Made Him carry the cross
On the wounds He bore.

At a place called Golgatha
A multitude gathered 'round
To watch Him be stripped
Nailed to the cross and bound.

I know He forgave them
They know not what they do
But those who felt remorse
Were surprisingly few.

He rose to the Kingdom of Heaven
Just as He said He would
No other can fill His shoes
For being pure and good.

He can grant salvation
To those who believe
In what He said and did
And are willing to receive.

Dear Lord, I bow down
To worship at Your feet
I pray I measure up
To expectations I should meet.

I pray I can be tolerant
And as forgiving as You
I pray I can be loving
As deeply as You do.

I pray I can share the light
With others just like me
Who need Your guidance
To be all they can be.

I know the prophesy
Had to be fulfilled
But oh so merciless
The way He was killed.

Come Pray With Others

Steeple bells are ringing out
From the little church on the hill
Come learn about Jesus
And fulfill God's will.

Come pray with others
Who believe as you do
Listen to the choir
As you sit in the pew.

Sing out with gusto
The hymns from the book
It's not about
The way you look.

Hear the message
So long ago written
It won't take long
Before you're smitten.

For Jesus was and is
A beautiful being
He's worth the time
Of knowing and seeing.

God's Love In Prayer

& Thought

How Do I Talk To The Lord?

How do I talk to the Lord
What do I say?
Can I just tell Him
All about my day?

Do I talk to Him out loud
Or in a soft hushed tone?
Will He hear me weep
Will He hear me moan?

Will He think I'm weak
If I begin by crying?
Does it really matter
As long as I am trying?

Will He really care
If the words aren't just so?
Will He be there for me
Understand and know?

Will He think I'm silly
If I begin with a laugh?
Not knowing what to say
But on the right path?

Will doors be opened
Which once were closed?
Will questions be answered
Which now are posed?

Should I thank Him continually
For all He's done?
Even though my life
Hasn't been all fun.

Should I talk to Him every day
Or maybe once a week?
When things are going good
Or only when they're bleak?

Should I talk for a long time
Or keep it short and sweet?
Should I be a regular caller
Or only as a treat?

The point is to talk to Him
Not worry what to say
Feel the friendship and love
There should be no delay.

A Prayer For Help

Dear Lord
Help us be more like You
Help us say the right things
And do what You would do.

Help us be more patient
When things don't go our way
Give us a cheerful smile
At the end of a tiring day.

Help us be more understanding
Of others' needs to grow
Help us plant fruitful seeds
Of truth for them to know.

Help us be more loving
Of nations one and all
Help us ready our ears
To listen for Your call.

Help us open our eyes
To all the gifts You give
Help us open our hearts
So we can truly live.

Help us be more forgiving
Of those who do us wrong
Help us find direction
Of where we must belong.

Help us show the way
To the next generation
Help us prepare the day
For Your coming celebration.

Oh, dear Lord, help us
Be like You back then
Thank you for this day
And our daily bread, Amen.

A Prayer For Guidance

Dear Lord
Guide us to Your perfect light
Illuminate the pathway
Show us wrong from right.

Lead us not into temptation
Nor let us go astray
Keep us close by Your side
Don't let us drift away.

Take our hand in Yours, Lord
Let us feel Your love within
Feel compassion for our souls
And wash away our sin.

Decipher the roadmap
Shown in the Holy Book
Let us understand
The road You walked and took.

Oh, dear Lord, guide us
Draw us close to Your light
Let us bask in the brilliance
Where it's shining so bright.

Let a fraction of the rays
Penetrate our soul
Carrying us onward
To our destiny, our goal.

Show us Your footprints
Where You walked the road
Tell us more parables
And the seeds You sowed.

Enlighten our heads
As well as our hearts
Begin with the history
And where it all starts.

Take us on a journey
Through Biblical ages
Passage of time
Through all of the stages.

Review our life
Of what went wrong
Of where we were weak
And where we were strong.

Envelope us, dear Lord
With Your warmth and love
Guide us to the stairway
To Your home above.

Thank you, Lord
For hearing us today
Thank you for giving us
Another day to pray.

Pray In Earnest

Wrapped in a cocoon
Constrictively tight
Forced into darkness
Oblivious to light.

Restrictions on movement
Not able to speak
Kept in the shadows
Subdued and meek.

Resigned to submission
Feelings of neglect
Bruises on the inside
No one can detect.

Rays of hope
Seem all but nil
Except for God
Who loves you still.

Pray in earnest
With all your might
That He may hear
And answer your plight.

Receive His strength
To burst the cocoon
It's never too late
And never too soon.

Unfold those wings
And get ready to fly
Soar to the rooftops
Or mountains so high.

It's your turn to sparkle
With brand new wings
Carrying you afar
To whatever life brings.

Don't die restricted
Whether imagined or real
Don't compromise
How you actually feel.

Grasp onto God's love
In the depths of your heart
Hold on tightly
Nevermore to ever part.

Be Glad In Your Being

Why do people in affluent countries
Have a lack of appreciation
When in a snap it could be gone
And they'd be forced into deprivation.

God gave pure water, clean air
And trees bearing fruit were planted
But now even basic needs
And existence are taken for granted.

Communication with God
Has floundered over the years
And much of what He says
Has fallen on deaf ears.

The only way He can prove
He's still in command
Is when devastation hits
He reaches out a hand.

Not only should we thank Him
For each breath of every day
But we should be glad in our being
And living the Christian way.

I Pray, Dear Lord

I pray, dear Lord
Please keep my body strong
To help me through the tough times
When weaknesses come along.

I pray, dear Lord
Please keep my devotion strong
Protect my precious loved ones
Family lineage of whom I belong.

I pray, dear Lord
Please keep my faith in You strong
Provide me with the confidence
With Your help, I can do no wrong.

I pray, dear Lord
Please keep my hope for peace strong
Let all mankind join together
Let us sing the unity song.

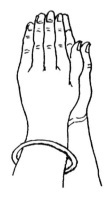

Always Remembered

I went to check on her that day
Opened the door just a crack
I could see her reclined in bed
With pillows behind her back.

She lay there so peacefully
Not a muscle did stir
Time had taken its toll
There was nothing more for her.

I drew closer to the bedside
To interpret the lines in her face
To understand the hardships
Of another time and place.

Homesteads on the prairies
Horse and buckboards travel mode
Physical toil till exhaustion
Trying to endure the heavy load.

No convenience items
Everything made from scratch
From the clothing they wore
To planting a garden patch.

Survival was the goal
Away back then
Winter taking its revenge
On the hardiest of men.

But somehow this robust woman
That I lay my eyes upon
Had survived the severe struggle
And now soon would be gone.

Her steady even breathing
And rhythmic heart will cease
Calmed by the Lord in Heaven
Giving her life a new lease.

She certainly deserves
A rest from the soil
Her hands tell the story
Contorted from toil.

Let me memorize her features
One last time in my head
As I cover the final pages
Of her legend I've read.

Her saga will live on
For generations to come
The stories repeated
Will be memories for some.

But to me I will remember
Her kind and thoughtful way
And how she looked so peaceful
On that warm summer's day.

Appreciate Silence

As I grow older
I value silence more
The quietness to hear
A pin drop on the floor.

The tranquil hush
Of a new day at dawn
The stillness of motion
Of dew on the lawn.

A mountain top feeling
Void of sound
Elements in harmony
Inner peace found.

Lost in my thoughts
Serenity unyielding
Solitude taking precedence
Confidence wielding.

Is it too much to ask
This busy world of noise
To stop the barking dogs
Control boisterous boys.

The cavalcade of motor cars
Zooming past my door
Would be banned from this street
Along with the neighbors mower.

Whistles blowing, sirens wailing
Would be part and package
Replacing sound with silence
There would be no lackage.

Silently like falling snow
The earth engulfed with peace
Every being filled to contentment
All contention would cease.

The benefits of noiselessness
Are too many to mention
And to say it could solve problems
Would be no pretension.

I value silence more and more
The older I grow
And perhaps it's a sign of wisdom
The more I learn and know.

Thinking Of You

As I was sitting by my window
Thinking of you today
What friendships join together
Doesn't seem so far away.

For when I think of you
Vivid visions in my mind
I think of someone special
Who's gentle, sweet and kind.

You're the type of friend
Most readily sought
With spiritual qualities
That can't be bought.

Although there's many miles
That keep us far apart
You're visited regularly
If only in my heart.

Thank You Dear Lord

Thank you dear Lord
For this beautiful day
Thank you for hearing
Every time I pray.

Thank you for answering
My every request
Thank you for knowing
What is the best.

Thank you for giving
Knowledge to learn
Thank you for waiting
While I discern.

Thank you for granting
The freedom to choose
Thank you for helping
So I seldom lose.

Thank you for loving
The way You do
Thank you for dieing
Giving salvation too.

Through The Window Inside

Try looking deep inside
Through the window of your heart
I know there's many layers
But this will be a start.

It may take some time
And involve a lot of pain
But it will be worth it
You've got so much to gain.

Get rid of dead issues
Deal with the past
Forgive yourself of errors
Love from within at last.

Make amends with others
If only in your mind
It's better to pardon
Than to despise, you'll find.

There's many types of love
From spiritual to passion
Love is abundant
No need to ration.

If your heart has been hardened
Try making the first move
Show a little kindness
Open up to prove.

That you're a good person
Even if actions say you're not
You just want to be loved
For the qualities you've got.

I know it's not easy
To change from the past
But it can be gradual
Doesn't need to be fast.

For a little loving
Can go a long way
It can cheer someone up
And make their day.

So try looking deep
Through that window inside
Pull out all the stops
Don't let all that love hide,

A Little Prayer For You

I say a little prayer for you
Every day of my life
I am your friend and confidante
Your lover, your wife.

In my prayer I thank God
For bringing you to me
I know in my heart of hearts
It was meant to be.

I pray for your safety
And all 'round protection
I wouldn't want anything
To destroy our connection.

I pray for your health
And spiritual strength
So we can be together
To go the full length.

I will continue the prayer
Every day of my life
For you, my darling
As long as I'm your wife.

Greatness & Gratitude

Greatness is walking away from a disagreement
and not having to be right.

Greatness is letting someone go on and on
about their accomplishments
and staying quiet about your own.

Greatness is giving, without any thought
of getting in return.

Greatness is spending time with someone infirmed
even though your schedule is fully booked.

Greatness is reaching out to someone
who is starved for love and affection.

Greatness is suffering without complaint.

Greatness is putting someone else's needs
before your own.

Greatness is having Jesus in your life.

Gratitude is waking up each morning
and being glad to be alive.

Gratitude is sharing memories of times
that touched your life.

Gratitude is being thankful for the bad experiences
in your life as well as the good.

Gratitude is realizing there are more good
people than bad.

Gratitude is fulfilling your purpose in life.

Gratitude is sharing your talents with others.

Gratitude is either giving or getting
a second chance.

Gratitude is having Jesus in your life.

God's Love Everlasting

In The Beginning

God created the heavens and earth
Stating, "Let there be light."
Dividing it from the darkness
Calling the darkness, Night.

He called the light, Day
And the firmament above, Heaven
He defined the waters, and days
Numbering from one to seven.

He called the dry land, Earth
Gathering the waters He called Seas
Then brought forth grass, herbs, seeds
And finally fruit bearing trees.

Then God created the Sun, the Moon
And the stars in the heavens above
They marked time and seasons
And He did it all with love.

On the fifth day He created
Great sea creatures and every winged bird
Saying, "Be fruitful and multiply,"
And it was God's word.

God brought forth the living creatures
Cattle and beasts according to its kind
Then made man in His own image
And gave him a ruling mind.

God blessed male and female
Dominion over fish, bird and beast
But gave seeds, herbs and fruits
To eat as their daily feast.

And on the seventh day
God decided to take a rest
He was pleased with His creation
For He knew it was His best.

According To Luke

And so it was written
In the days of yore
He said to His disciples
Blessed are you the poor.

Blessed are you that hunger
For you shall hunger no more
Blessed are you that weep now
For you shall weep neither nor.

Blessed are you that are hated
In the Son of God's name
For your reward is great in Heaven
As the prophets before came.

I say, love your enemies
Do good to those who hate
Bless those who curse you
And who unduly spate.

To him who strikes one cheek
The other available make
Nor withhold your tunic to him
As well as your cloak to take.

Give to everyone who asks
But never ask for goods back
Treat everyone as thyself wish
And therefore be no lack.

If you love only who love you
Even sinners the same do
If you do good only to the good
What credit is that to you?

Love your enemies, do good, lend
Hope for nothing in return
You will be sons of the Most High
And your reward great to learn.

Judge not, He said
You shall not be judged the same
Condemn not
And you shall not take the blame.

Forgive
And you will be forgiven
Give
And unto you it will be given.

This Place Called Heaven

We come into this world
All naked and bare
We go out of this realm
With nary a care.

Where there is no dawning
And no setting sun
Where there is no currency
Or menial work done.

Where there's no fast food outlets
Or fancy hot rod cars
Where there's no casinos
Or noisy pubs or bars.

Where the grass is always green
And the flowers always flourish
Where souls live in harmony
And never act boorish.

Where body image isn't important
But self-esteem is number one
Where being humble is an asset
Loving others is next to none.

Where the weather is constant
No extreme up or downs
Where beautiful music plays
And there's no unpleasant sounds.

Where Jesus surrounded by children
Is dressed in His robe of white
His little lambs eager to follow
His path of goodness and right.

This place called Heaven
Where we come before God
Let's pray we are accepted
And get the approving nod.

In A Perfect World

If we lived in a perfect world
There'd be no wars, no brawls
There'd be no fighting
And there'd be no boundary walls.

If we lived in a perfect world
Every day would be bright
Nothing would be wrong
Everything would be right.

If we lived in a perfect world
No pollution in the air
No health problems or diseases
And everyone treated fair.

If we lived in a perfect world
There'd be no hassle in traffic
Communications would be a breeze
Everyone would be telepathic.

If we lived in a perfect world
Flowers would bloom non-stop
All animals would play together
And love would be over-the-top.

If we lived in a perfect world
Sweet music would fill our ears
We'd feel safe and secure
Never have any doubts or fears.

We don't live in a perfect world
But I know who does
He came to us from up above
The greatest Man who was.

He told us of this perfect world
With His Father and He
There'd be eternal life
For you and for me.

In this perfect world
We won't be all stressed
It will be tranquility
A place our soul will rest.

Look forward to our perfect world
Although it isn't here
We can't see or touch it now
But it's where we'll be freer.

Conquer The Fear

The fear of leaving
Is painfully real
Not knowing what's beyond
Or what's in the deal.

Is there really a Heaven
Is there life after death
Can we have one more life
Or one more bequeath?

Will we be all alone
Or meet others we knew
Will there be lots of people
Or surprisingly few?

Will we be enveloped by darkness
Or blasted by light
Plunged into oblivion
Or gain added sight?

Will we recall life's events
Of what went on before
In centuries past
From now forever more?

Will we come before God
Or maybe His Son
Will we try to explain
All the errs we've done?

Will He forgive us
Our sins to unfold
Will they be washed away
Just as we were told?

Will it help to bow down
Oh, what will I say
When I meet my maker
On that fateful day.

Why didn't I try harder
To do things more right
He'd maybe be more willing
To hear my final plight.

The Bible gives us insight
Of what is to come
Peace, love and harmony
For all, not just some.

So how can we be sure
What lies beyond the bend
Are we getting the right signals
Of what He wants to send?

That's when faith steps in
Can be felt deep inside
Trust feelings of the heart
Let the Lord be your guide.

Be carried to freedom
Beyond earthly ways
To eternal love
To glorious days.

God Loves You

God loves you
In so many ways
He's there to guide you
Through difficult days.

He knows your inner being
And how you must feel
He knows when you hurt
And when you must heal.

He knows when you're tired
And when you must rest
He gives you the choices
But He knows what's best.

He has the master plan
But lets you go your way
He's there for you at work
And there for you at play.

Trust in God
Reach out for His protection
Yield to His guidance
Have a spiritual connection.

Another's Loss

I can't begin to know the pain
Another's going through
I can't begin to know
What to say to them or do.

Loss of another is personal
It affects in different ways
Sometimes everything's okay
Then there are horrible days.

The unpredictable emotions
Of the ups and downs
Can bring fits of laughter
Then change quickly to frowns.

The feeling of loneliness sets in
Even in a sea of faces
Some days it's difficult
To go through daily paces.

The sense of a loved one
Taken away – never coming back
Is enough in some minds
To make a person crack.

Just like other obstacles
It takes one day at a time
One foot in front of the other
To make bad days become fine.

Never give up hope
Of feeling peace within
Drawing on a spiritual force
Is where we should begin.

For the love of Jesus
Is always at our side
Waiting for us to call on Him
If we can push away our pride.

Losing A Child

There's no greater loss
Than losing a child
Inside feels empty
Cheated and beguiled.

Such promise
Now gone, taken away
Thoughts of their presence
Every minute of the day.

Death feels so final
But really it's not
Faith believes eternity
In our hearts deeply sought.

Loss is a wound
The pain is real
The deeper the cut
The longer to heal.

Words cannot help
Only love from within
But where do we start
Where do we begin?

Thank God for creation
Of body and soul
When the body's no longer
Then Heaven's the goal.

Thank God for time together
Fleeting like a loan
Would have been more loving
If only had we known.

Thank God for precious gifts
A child being one
No finer creation
Could ever be done.

Thank God for eternal life
Peace of mind at hand
Knowing He loves us
Like each grain of sand.

God knows how we feel
He gave His only Son
And when we turn to Him
Our life's just begun.

I've Just Lost A Loved One

I've just lost a loved one
It hasn't been that long
I feel so all alone
Like I don't really belong.

Like a circle's been broken
And the ends don't meet
Even the smallest tasks
Seem like a major feat.

I stay awake all night
And want to sleep all day
People try to help
But they don't know what to say.

I just want my life back
The way it was before
For the pain to go away
To be happy once more.

I know that's unrealistic
To ask for that as such
But surely God knows
I loved them so much.

Why has this happened to me
Am I the only one
Maybe they'd still be here
If different things were done.

I wish I'd spent more time
Saying I loved them so
Or just holding their hand
Just to let them know.

But now I'm all alone
The feeling won't go away
If I could bring them back
I'd do it right today.

Other days I get so angry
They aren't here with me
I think of how it was
Now how it has to be.

I think I'm going crazy
Totally losing my mind
I see their face in everyone
But it's not them – I find.

Everything reminds me
Even the songs they play
Memories keep coming back
Haunting me day after day.

What can I do Lord
To get me past this
To find happiness again
To truly find bliss.

Let the Lord heal
All the aches and pains
Open your heart
For spiritual gains.

Let the Lord deal with
The problems at hand
Listen to His guidance
And His loving command.

Let the Lord wash away
Your sins and mine
Be devoted to Him
Everlasting divine.

Weep For Me No More

I have journeyed the road of life
Weep for me no more at my passing
For the Lord is gathering His flock
Every creed, color and race He's amassing.

I have traveled the valleys and the peaks
Have put my heart into it all
He has been there for me with guidance
Whether I stood upright or took a fall.

So I go to Heaven with Him willingly
With my body erect and head held high
I have fulfilled my earthly purpose
Now it is time to bid everyone goodbye.

But weep for me no more at my passing
We will meet again in another place
Where time stretches into eternity
And where we all come to God's good grace.

I Couldn't Keep Him Waiting

I had to go with the Lord so suddenly
I didn't have time to personally say goodbye
I wanted to give you one last hug
But I couldn't keep Him waiting or ask why.

I wanted to tell you how much I loved you
How being together gave me such a high
But everything was happening so rapidly
And I couldn't keep Him waiting or ask why.

I wanted to give you one last kiss
Breath filling my lungs with one deep sigh
Then I was drawn away on a journey
Because I couldn't keep Him waiting or ask why.

I didn't mean for my departure to be abrupt
Some say that's what we do when we die
But I knew I had to be with Him
For He was waiting and I couldn't ask why.

I'm With The Lord Now

The Lord held His hand out
Beckoning me to come with Him
I knew I couldn't say no
This was much more than a whim.

He offered me peace I'd never known
In my heart I knew it was best
For the days of toil were gone
And it was time for my body to rest.

I put my trust in His guidance
To know what was best for me
Letting His unconditional love
Carry me through eternity.

Know that I'm with the Lord now
He held His hand out for mine
Someday we'll be together again
In another place and time.

My Path Was Not Always Easy

My path was not always easy
There were bumps along the way
But my belief in Jesus
Helped me through the day.

He was there in my rising up
And there when I took a fall
He's here for me again
When I answered His call.

My time was too short
I have to agree it's true
But when God calls us home
Our work here is through.

No need to feel sad, my friends
Don't worry 'bout me, my love
For I'm in good company
With all the angels above.

Acknowledgements

My life has not always been easy but I know since I have accepted Jesus into my heart, it has steadily climbed upward. I give complete credit of my successes to Him.

Distribution across Western Canada I accredit to the forty years direct sales experience my husband, Verne, contributes to our small publishing company. We enjoy meeting people from all walks of life – from flower shops, country drug stores, hospital gift shops to funeral homes and libraries – as we travel north, south, east and west. Thank you for opening your doors to us and allowing God's light to shine forth for all to see.

Thank you to Jan a gifted artist, who created the illustrations and covers for six of my books. A special thank you to Ashraf the first person I spoke to about an idea of putting a bunch of poems together to make a book. That was nine years and nine books ago (the first *You Mean The World To Me* was revised sporting a new cover and illustrations). Ashraf has always allowed his professionalism to be top priority in the printing of quality work. I appreciate the talents these two men bring to me in helping produce a product many thousands of people can enjoy.

And lastly, thank you to you, the readers and supporters of my passion for writing, a huge embrace of love goes out to you. May the words and expressions of the poems within these covers, touch your lives in a loving and positive way.

About the Author

Elaine was born and raised in the Edmonton, Alberta area, attending school at Campbelltown, Sherwood Park, Colchester and Salisbury High.

Inspiration to write poetry began when Elaine, as a young woman of twenty-nine, started reading a children's Bible given to her daughter as a birthday gift. It made her look at life in a whole new manner. Her thoughts became revealed in rhyming verse.

Besides writing poetry and prose, the author enjoys traveling, photography, ballroom dancing, aerobics, hiking, decorating and live theatre.

Elaine has two grown children; Tammy and Kyle. Husband Verne and her reside in Edmonton, Alberta during the summer months and spend the winters in warmer climates.